Amnesty International
proudly present

The Secret Policeman's Other Ball

Edited by Martin Lewis & Peter Walker
Photography by Adrian Boot & Michael Putland
Art Direction by Derek Birdsall

Programme Notes by Terry Jones and Michael Palin

Methuen

Please note:

A Note About the Programme Notes by Jones and Palin

Many of you - some of you - well, Michael's mother will have doubtless noticed that we were not in the show itself. Indeed this is the first Amnesty thing that one or other of us hasn't been in. Now we don't want any nasty rumours going around that we were afraid to share a dressingroom with Pamela Stephenson or that Terry has joined the Chilean police force. The reason is simply that stars of our magnitude cannot be expected to drop everything and turn out, well after our bedtime to entertain a few thousand drunken insomniacs at a flea-pit like the Theatre Royal, Drury Lane (where you can't get to the bloody toilet for statues of old theatre managers). Both of us had heavy commitments during that week - Terry was in the middle of a course of penicillin and Michael was putting up a shelf.

However, Martin 'This one really *is* urgent' Lewis finally approached us to do the Programme Notes with an offer even we could not refuse. Six mint lumps. One on delivery of finished artwork, one on publication and four when sales reached 46 million. Our agent accepted the offer (and has since been transferred to the Death Valley office).

The notes that follow are intended to be plain honest observations on behalf of two people who weren't there and who are insanely jealous of anyone else's success.

Michael Palin and Terry Jones, Kentish Town Job Centre, October 1981

Programme

Show directed by Ronald Eyre
Assisted by John Cleese
Photography by Adrian Boot & Michael Putland
Programme notes by Terry Jones & Michael Palin

Bugging it possible sack.

A Word of Thanks (*Rowan Atkinson, John Cleese & Ronald Eyre*)	**The company**
Overture (*Ludwig van Beethoven; arr. Rowan Atkinson*)	**Rowan Atkinson**
Chekhov and the Gorilla (*John Bird & John Fortune*)	**John Bird** **John Fortune** **Chris Langham**
French Lessons I Song in a French Accent (*Neil Innes*)	**Neil Innes**
II Une Drama Française (*Rory McGrath & Jimmy Mulville*)	**Griff Rhys Jones & friends**
A Religious Experience (*Chris Langham*)	**Chris Langham**
Beekeeping (*At Last the 1948 Show: Tim Brooke-Taylor,* *Graham Chapman, John Cleese, Marty Feldman*)	**Rowan Atkinson** **John Cleese**
What's On in Stoke Newington (*Alexei Sayle*)	**Alexei Sayle**
Death on the Roads I Australian Motor Insurance Claims (*Jasper Carrott*)	**Jasper Carrott**
II Road Safety (*traditional; arr. Rowan Atkinson*)	**Rowan Atkinson**
The Royal Australian Prostate Foundation (*Barry Humphries*)	**Dame Edna Everage**

★ ★ ★

Musical Interlude

The Universal Soldier (*Buffy Sainte-Marie*)	. . . . . .	Donovan
I Don't Like Mondays (*Bob Geldof*)	. . . . . .	Johnny Fingers & Bob Geldof
Farther Up the Road . (*Don Robey & Joe Veasey*)	. . . . . .	Jeff Beck & Eric Clapton
In the Air Tonight (*Phil Collins*)	. . . . . .	Phil Collins
Message in a Bottle (*Sting*)	. . . . . .	Sting
Roxanne . (*Sting*)	. . . . . .	Sting

★ ★ ★

Top of the Form (*John Cleese*)	. . . . . .	Rowan Atkinson John Bird Tim Brooke-Taylor Graham Chapman John Cleese John Fortune Griff Rhys Jones

Sorry, but this is the 13th time John Cleese's name has been mentioned and we're only on page 3. →

I've Had It Up to Here With Men (*Victoria Wood*)	. . . .	Victoria Wood
Divorce Service . (*John Cormack*)	. . . . . .	Rowan Atkinson John Fortune Griff Rhys Jones Pamela Stephenson
Denis and Ronnie (*John Wells*)	. . . . . .	John Wells
Clothes Off! . (*At Last the 1948 Show: Tim Brooke-Taylor,* *Graham Chapman, John Cleese, Marty Feldman*)	. . . . . .	Graham Chapman John Cleese Pamela Stephenson
Alan and John . (*Alan Bennett*)	. . . . . .	Alan Bennett John Fortune
Drinking . (*Billy Connolly*)	. . . . . .	Billy Connolly
Finale I Shall Be Released (*Bob Dylan*)	. . . .	The Secret Police

A word of thanks...

Before the performance all the cast are on stage. JOHN CLEESE addresses the audience.

JOHN CLEESE. Ladies and gentlemen, before we start the show this evening we do just want to take this opportunity of expressing on behalf of Amnesty our sincerest thanks to you for being with us tonight. I am sure that you will be thrilled to know that tonight's house has raised the truly magnificent sum of seventeen thousand five hundred and sixty pounds. Thank you. And in particular we want to say a special word of thanks to all of you down here who paid the rather splendid price of twelve pounds fifty a ticket. Incidentally, I am sure all the rest of you will be interested to know that had you all paid twelve pounds fifty tonight we would have raised over fifty-two thousand pounds. But nevertheless we do, really do, want to thank each and every one of you, even those of you right up the top there who only paid the . . . well, the bare minimum of six pounds. Thank you.

CHRIS LANGHAM. Three pounds fifty.
JOHN CLEESE. What?
CHRIS LANGHAM. It's only three pounds fifty at the very top.
JOHN CLEESE. You are joking . . . You bastards. I mean you . . . People are being tortured to death all over the world and you're prepared to cough up the price of two prawn cocktails. I mean, aren't you ashamed of yourselves – gatecrashing a . . . charity event like this when public figures like us – person-alities – whose very urine samples are of national importance, give our services completely free, for absolutely nothing, not a miserable . . . Never mind, never mind . . . I don't want to spoil the atmosphere. Ladies and gentlemen, I did want to thank all of you – or most of you anyway – and now on with the show. Ladies and gentlemen, we kick off tonight with Mr Rowan At –

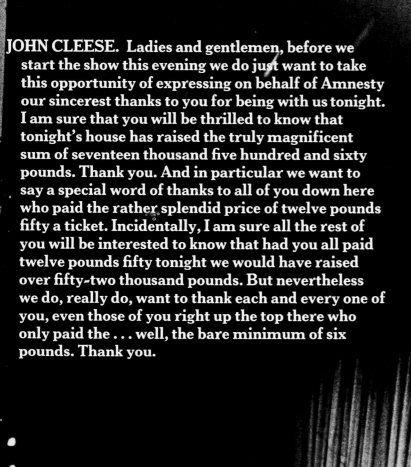

JOHN BIRD. On the other hand, let's not forget that the people up there are after all the casualties of our society . . . students, people gassed in the war, hospital porters . . .

DAVID RAPPAPORT. Dwarfs.

JOHN BIRD. Dwarfs.

PAMELA STEPHENSON. Lesbians.

JOHN BIRD. Lesbians, exactly . . . so although they have only paid three pounds fifty, let's not forget they've had to save up for tonight, this is their big splash for the year and they've at least paid for it out of their own pockets, whereas the people down here are, let's face it, writing this off against tax.

JOHN CLEESE. Really?

JOHN BIRD. Oh, yes. How many people down here have actually paid for your own tickets? See . . . none.

JOHN CLEESE. You miserable cheapskates . . . Anyway, on with the show, have fun . . . ladies and gentlemen . . . Mr Rowan Atkin –

ROWAN ATKINSON. Actually, the ones who really get up my nose are those people who buy the second cheapest seats, the people who always buy the second cheapest wine in the restaurant just to show their girlfriends they're not part of the "oi polloi" up there. I mean, I agree with you. Who wants to sit next to someone in jeans? And you lot underneath them, who'd like to be down here with the rich and influential, but are too flabby to pay top whack, you're the indecisive, wishy-washy, gutless middle-of-the-road, sitting on every fence –

ALAN BENNETT. They're the fucking Social Democrats.

Whole cast make rude gestures to middle two tiers.

JOHN CLEESE. And now . . . on with the show, ladies and gentlemen, Rowan Atkinson.

Overture

Welcome to page 7.
Specially dedicated to
the slow reader.

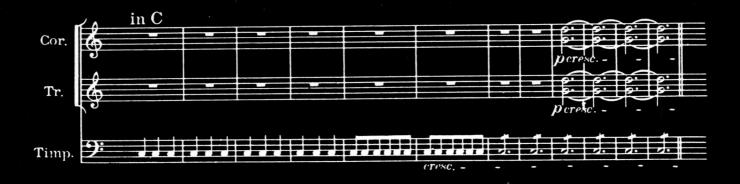

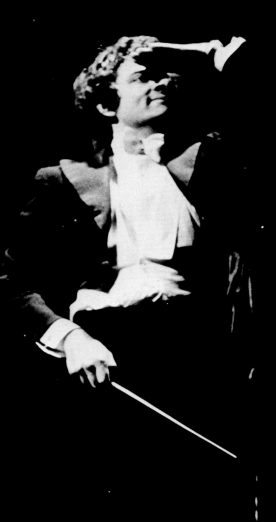

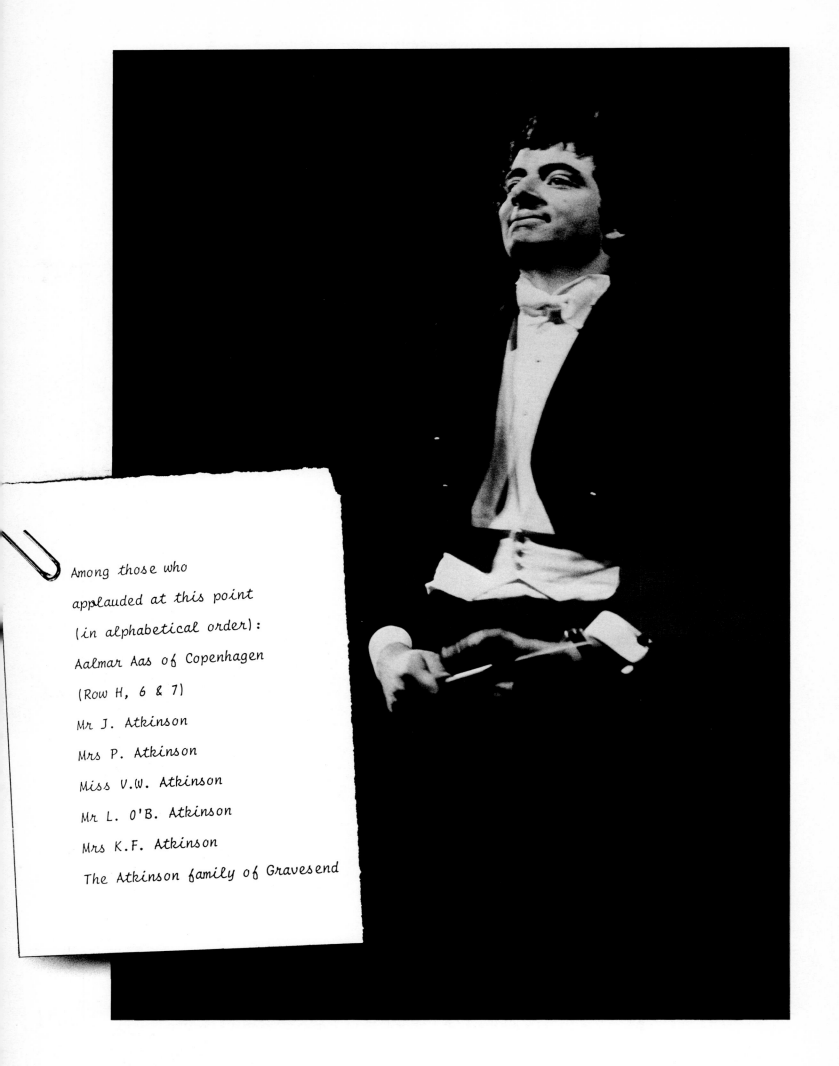

Among those who
applauded at this point
(in alphabetical order):
Aalmar Aas of Copenhagen
(Row H, 6 & 7)
Mr J. Atkinson
Mrs P. Atkinson
Miss V.W. Atkinson
Mr L. O'B. Atkinson
Mrs K.F. Atkinson
The Atkinson family of Gravesend

Chekhov & The Gorilla

Also available in this series:

The Chimpanzee Orchard

The Three Primates

The Seagull - Forerunner of Man?

Me Tarzan - You Uncle Vanya

METHUEN FOR MONKEYS series

In the latter years of the nineteenth century a revolution took place in European drama. At the forefront of this new movement was the Moscow Art Theatre. In the following scene we see a meeting of the board of directors of the Moscow Art Theatre after the first preview of 'The Cherry Orchard'. Present are Anton Chekhov, the playwright, Constantin Stanislavski, the director, and the financial director of the theatre, Sergei Nemirovich.

STANISLAVSKI. I thought, you know, that Cherry Orchard went pretty well, Anton.

CHEKHOV. Not bad, not bad.

STANISLAVSKI. I mean, especially, you know, for a first preview. I think, you know, you've really answered the critics who say you can't write a happy ending.

CHEKHOV. Oh, yeah, yeah.

STANISLAVSKI. I mean, the characters always end up in despair or shooting themselves or whatever. I think you certainly got away from that with the big production number at the end. Very upbeat. I just have this worry at the back of my mind that when all the characters come on at the end –

CHEKHOV. Yeah.

STANISLAVSKI. – and go into the song (Sings.) 'The orchard is saved –'

CHEKHOV. Yeah, yeah, Good number.

STANISLAVSKI. – then go into the big dance number and throw the streamers into the audience –

CHEKHOV. And the bubble machine.

STANISLAVSKI. – I just have this slight feeling that it doesn't quite gel with the general atmosphere of what's gone before. Do you know what I mean?

CHEKHOV. I know what you mean. Yeah, there is a bit of a change of gear at that point.

STANISLAVSKI. Right. I mean, I wouldn't like to lose any of the sort of pizzaz or the optimism or sending the audience home in a happy mood. I just wondered if we could do a bit of fine tuning at the end of the play.

CHEKHOV. Well, I was thinking about this last night, actually, Constantin, and I've come up with something which might just fit the bill. Now, this is all off the top of my head, a bit rough and all that. But let's say, for the purposes of argument, let's say the orchard isn't saved.

STANISLAVSKI. Isn't saved?

CHEKHOV. Isn't saved.

STANISLAVSKI. Now, don't forget what the critics say about your doomy endings.

CHEKHOV. No, hang about. So all the characters are a bit pissed off about that, they all come in, and the

old lady comes on and she's a bit tearful, like we all would be. Looks around and says goodbye house, goodbye chairs, goodbye light fittings, goodbye fire extinguisher, you know, goodbye whatever. And she goes off and the stage is empty. Now you remember that bloke who was on in the first two acts, the old servant, what was his name?

STANISLAVSKI. Firs.

CHEKHOV. Firs. That's the fellow. Now he went down well, a very lovable eccentric character.

STANISLAVSKI. Dynamite.

CHEKHOV. Got a lot of laughs. Now the audience hasn't seen him for, what, half an hour? So he's been locked away in a cupboard somewhere, he comes out, has a look round the stage, goes about muttering to himself about they've all gone off and left him and his life's passed him by without him noticing and all that caper, and he sits down, twanging noise and the curtain comes down. How about that?

STANISLAVSKI. I like it, Anton. I think it could work.

CHEKHOV. I mean, what you've got there, Constantin, you've got your humour . . .

STANISLAVSKI. You've got your humour, you've got your pathos going on. You've got the best of both worlds. What do you think, Sergei Nemirovich?

SERGEI NEMIROVICH. Yes, yes, I think I see what you're driving at there. It sort of rounds off the play more. Yes, I go along with that.

STANISLAVSKI. Good, good, right.

SERGEI NEMIROVICH. There is one slight suggestion that I would make. It's just a small point really.

STANISLAVSKI. What's that, then, Sergei Nemirovich?

SERGEI NEMIROVICH. It is only a suggestion. Shoot me down in flames if you think I'm barking up the wrong tree here. How would it be, during, as an example sort of thing, during the time that the old servant was off stage and locked in the cupboard or wherever he happens to be, how would it be if, during that intervening period of time, he could have been somehow, by some means or other, don't ask me exactly how, sort of . . . changed . . . transformed into something different, if he could be changed . . . into a gorilla.

CHEKHOV. I knew it, I knew it would be something like that. Jesus wept.

STANISLAVSKI. Calm down, Anton.

CHEKHOV. For Christ's sake. That's all I get, that's all he ever wants. Gorillas, gorillas, gorillas. Why can't we have a gorilla in the play? Why can't two gorillas be at the dinner party? Why can't a gorilla bring on the samovar? What the fuck's he talking about? Changing a servant into a gorilla. What's he trying to do?

SERGEI NEMIROVICH. Pardon me for breathing. I'm only the financial director.

CHEKHOV. What the fuck's the matter with him? Let me just remind you what we're trying to do in this theatre. We're trying to create a new revolutionary naturalistic kind of drama, where the audience can come in, they can sit in the audience, they can look at the stage and they can identify with the characters on the stage, they can see their own ordinary, humdrum lives being portrayed with honesty, with truthfulness, with realism. Let me just ask you this one simple question. How many, exactly what proportion of the audience that comes to the Moscow Art Theatre every night, are in fact gorillas?

SERGEI NEMIROVICH. Well, I come every night for one.

CHEKHOV. Of course you fucking come, you're the financial director. You get free bloody seats.

SERGEI NEMIROVICH. Well of course I get free seats. Where am I going to put a ticket stub?

CHEKHOV. The same place you put your banana.

SERGEI NEMIROVICH. Oh, that's very nice. I see the way the conversation is sliding now. I wondered when you'd come out from under your stone, Anton. Let's face it; you don't actually like gorillas, do you?

CHEKHOV. I wouldn't say that, I've got nothing against gorillas. I just don't think the stage is the right place to have a gorilla, actually.

Look at that face.
Now why didn't John Bird get
the lead in <u>Robert Hardy:</u>
<u>The Wilderness Years</u>? He
looks much more like him
than Churchill

French Lessons

SONG IN A FRENCH ACCENT

I like to keep alive the international flavour for this Amnesty evening. I would like to sing you a song in French, or at least in a French accent. This song has been specially arranged for me for one guitar and one donkey. This is the guitar – and this is the donkey.

WHAT THE CRITICS SAID ABOUT NEIL INNES:

'Neil Innes brings that rare quality of absolute genius to everything he does.'

Mid-Suffolk Herald

'Neil Innes brings that rare quality of absolute total genius to everything he does.'

Mid-Suffolk Herald (2nd edition)

'If Neil Innes were a footballer he'd surely have scored all three goals in Saturday's match against Middlesborough.'

Mid-Suffolk Herald (sports page)

'Neil's begonias are worth travelling miles to see.'

Mid-Suffolk Herald (gardening section)

FOR SALE: 1 Neil Innes concert ticket £350 o.n.o.

Mid-Suffolk Herald (small ads)

Neil, 22, hails from mid-Suffolk. His hobbies are falconry, phone installation, listening to Radio Hilversum and editing the local paper.

Hee-haw hee-haw
Hee-haw hee-haw
Hee-haw hee-haw
Hee-haw hee-haw
Hee-haw hee-haw
Hee-haw hee-haw
Hee-haw hee-haw

We have no time for lovers' games
Of hide-and-seek or cat-and-mouse
I come home tired, you call me names
You work all week at keeping house
I understand the drudgery
Of what you do but don't you think
The office is the same for me
You ask me to unblock the sink

Life is getting shorter
Nickel dime and quarter
Talk is getting cheaper
Love is getting deeper
Hee-haw hee-haw
Hee-haw hee-haw
Hee-haw hee-haw
Hee-haw hee-haw
Hee-haw hee-haw
Mitterrand

I get to work under the sink
I bang my head, the spanner slips
I cut my hand and wish I had a drink
But curse instead. The water drips
I raise my voice, you nag at me
The baby slides around the floor
You say 'Be quiet', I have no choice
The slightest noise disturbs next door

Life is getting shorter
Nickel dime and quarter
Talk is getting cheaper
Love is getting deeper
Hee-haw hee-haw
Hee-haw hee-haw
Hee-haw hee-haw
Hee-haw hee-haw
Hee-haw hee-haw
Hee-haw hee-haw
St Tropez

The kettle boils, the baby cries
I pick him up, his little teeth
Are coming through. I dry his eyes
You break a cup and underneath
The kitchen light your pretty face
Is close to tears and so my heart
Goes out to you as we embrace
Love reappears to play its part

Life is getting shorter
Nickel dime and quarter
Talk is getting cheaper
Love is getting deeper
Hee-haw hee-haw
Hee-haw hee-haw
Hee-haw hee-haw
Hee-haw hee-haw
Hee-haw hee-haw
Hee-haw hee-haw
Hee-haw hee-haw

UNE DRAMA FRANÇAISE

CAST

Le Gendarme	. . . .	Jimmy Mulville
Le Husband	. . . .	Martin Bergman
L'Autre Homme	. . .	Griff Rhys Jones
Frou Frou La Gorge	. .	Clive Anderson

LE GENDARME. Soir, all. Vous savez, un gendarme's lot n'est pas une heureuse une. Cette semaine, par example, j'étais sur le frappe quand nous avions un petit spot de trouble. C'était la même vieille histoire de la femme infidèle et le husband jaloux. La femme dans la question était une certaine Frou-Frou La Gorge, une jolie pièce de crackling, avec des bons frappeurs et une vrai cul de sac. Son husband était un professor de sociology and a boring old bugger to boot.

LE HUSBAND. Au revoir, chérie, je vais au travail.

LE GENDARME. Mais avant que tu puisse dire 'Jack Robinson', entre l'autre homme.

L'AUTRE HOMME (entering). Frou-Frou!

FROU-FROU. Ooooh! . . . (They embrace.)

LE GENDARME. Pendant cette hors d'oeuvre, cette petite pièce de cordon bleu, this little bit of how's your père, oui, vous avez guessed it.

LE HUSBAND (entering). J'arrive!

L'AUTRE HOMME. Merde! (Tries to hide under a chair.)

LE HUSBAND. Bonjour, chérie. Qu'est – ce que c'est que ça?

FROU-FROU. Quoi?

LE HUSBAND. Ne me donne 'quoi', salope. Qui est cet homme?

FROU-FROU. Quel homme?

LE HUSBAND. Le homme holding the chaise.

L'AUTRE HOMME. Bonjour!

LE HUSBAND. Bonjour!

L'AUTRE HOMME. All right, I admit it. Elle et moi, nous avons – l'affaire.

FROU-FROU
LE HUSBAND } Comment?

L'AUTRE HOMME. Elle et moi, nous avons un peu de anqui-panqui.

LE HUSBAND. Ah!

L'AUTRE HOMME. Oui, c'est vrai. Je l'aime.

LE HUSBAND. Tu l'aimes?

FROU-FROU. Il m'aime.

FROU-FROU
L'AUTRE HOMME } Nous nous aimons, vous vous
LE HUSBAND } aimez, ils s'aiment.

LE GENDARME. Le husband perdra son cool.

LE HUSBAND. Prends ça, toi. (He shoots.) Pan, pan et pan.

L'AUTRE HOMME. Aaah! Ugh! Eegh!

LE HUSBAND. Non, non, non, non. Répétez avec moi:

LE HUSBAND
L'AUTRE HOMME } A – e – i – o – u.

FROU-FROU. Je pense que . . . est-il . . .?

LE HUSBAND. Oui. Il est. Et toi. Prends ça! (Shoots her.)
(French sound effects.) Pin-pan-pin-pan-pin-pan –

LE HUSBAND. Merde! Les cochons!

LE GENDARME (aside). Et maintenant je entrais et caught him avec la main rouge. (To LE HUSBAND) 'Allo 'allo 'allo, qu'est-ce que nous avons ici, then?

LE HUSBAND. Monsieur l'officer, dis donc –

LE GENDARME. Je n'étais pas born hier, mate.

LE HUSBAND. Mais – c'est vrai je vous assure –

LE GENDARME. Coupez le crap et venez à la gare doucement, soleil-shine. (Aside.) Vous savez, quelques gens ne jamais learn. Peut-etre le société –

LE HUSBAND. La société.

LE GENDARME. – la société est dans la blame. Qui sait? Il y a un vieux French proverb qui dit, 'Si vous avez un peu de l'autre sur le side, ne dansez pas sur le pont d'Avignon without your socks on.' 'Nuit, all.

A Religious Experience

By Chris Langham who has spent nine years in a monastery and three quarters of an hour in a convent.

It's a very religious experience, of course, being in a
show like this. Bob Dylan and I have a lot in
common . . . we're both trying to get off religion and
back on to hard drugs.

Actually I don't use any stimulants. Apart from
cocaine. My doctor tells me I have to take cocaine.
Apparently I'm not getting enough salt. I don't know if
you've ever tried this, but if you sniff a lot of talcum
powder up your nose and then rub the insides of your
nostrils with very, very fine sandpaper, take about
twenty-five diet tablets (the very speedy kind), and
tear up a lot of money, it's exactly like taking cocaine!...

I come from a very rough neighbourhood so it's OK
if you want to rush the stage, that's fine by me. In fact,
a few weeks ago, when all the riots were on a guy came
round to my house and he said: 'There's going to be a
rumble this evening. Everybody bring pieces.'
I thought he said pizzas. So I turn up with this fucking
thing. There was this huge fight because there wasn't
enough to go round . . .

They're dumb guys round our neighbourhood,
white guys who go out looting in the daytime so they
can't be seen.

I don't get involved anymore . . . I used to be
politically involved. I was a member of an activist
wing of the Young Conservatives. We were called the
Moderate Terrorist Front. We were trying to bring
about a more moderate world, trying to instil a more
middle-of-the-road, reasonable attitude in people . . .
and we were prepared to kill and maim to achieve
this. The last terrorist act we pulled, we planted a fish
soup aboard a jumbo jet. And we told them. If it
wasn't eaten within twenty-four hours it would go off.
And it did.

We were going to have an escapologist on the show
tonight but unfortunately he couldn't get away. So
now what we're going to bring you instead is a dazzling
display of trapeze skills.

eekeeping

BEEKEEPING SKETCH

A Historical Note

This sketch was first performed at the
Dissolution of the Barebones Parliament.
It was revived by royal decree in 1521
and performed constantly during the
Tudor period. Under the Cromwellian
protectorate it was made an offence to
perform the sketch in public and two
young counter-performers from Ilford were
boiled alive as witches for doing it at a
'Save the Monarchy' charity show in 1659.
John Cleese found the sketch when cleaning
out some old drawers to look for material
for a new David Frost series.   He

INTERVIEWER. Good evening. Tonight we're taking a look at beekeeping, and here to tell us all about it we have in the studio a man who has been keeping bees for over forty years, Mr Reginald Prawnbaum. Good evening, Mr Prawnbaum.

PRAWNBAUM. Good evening.

INTERVIEWER. Tell me, what first interested you in the bee world, Mr Prawnbaum?

PRAWNBAUM. Well, even as a child I used to –

INTERVIEWER. SSH!

PRAWNBAUM. I'm sorry, shouldn't I have said that?

INTERVIEWER. No, of course you should. Pay no attention. When I say 'SSH' it's just a nervous mannerism I've picked up. If I want you to keep quiet I will say 'SHOOSH.' You were saying?

PRAWNBAUM. Oh, I see. Well, even as a child I used to wander around –

INTERVIEWER. SH!

PRAWNBAUM. – in the fields near my house watching bees flying from flower to flower –

INTERVIEWER. SH!

PRAWNBAUM. – and, er, taking note of the flowers that they visited.

INTERVIEWER. SHOOSH!

PRAWNBAUM. Was that wrong?

INTERVIEWER. I'm so sorry. Did I say 'SHOOSH?' I meant 'SSH.' Do go on, it's most interesting.

PRAWNBAUM. And so I have grown to love the little, er –

INTERVIEWER. SSH.

PRAWNBAUM. – creatures. You know, nature really has produced a little masterpiece in the life of the bee.

INTERVIEWER. QUARK! I'm sorry. I'm afraid that's a reflex action too. I squawk whenever someone mentions the word 'life'. QUARK! You see, even when I mention it myself. I should have told you. Please go on.

PRAWNBAUM. Oh, very well. Bees, as you know, are divided into –

INTERVIEWER. SSH!

PRAWNBAUM. – different categories –

INTERVIEWER. SSSH.

PRAWNBAUM. – the queen bee and the worker bee, whose life span –

INTERVIEWER. QUARK!

PRAWNBAUM. – whose living expectancy is only one year.

INTERVIEWER. SSH.

PRAWNBAUM. The worker bees, on the other hand, have a much longer –

INTERVIEWER. SHOOSH.

PRAWNBAUM. Do you want me to stop?

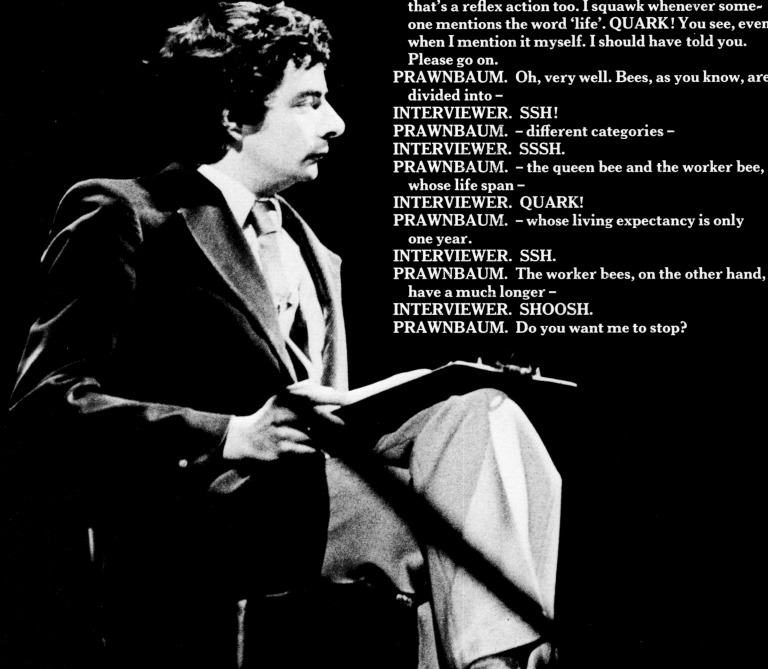

INTERVIEWER. Yes, you were about to say 'life'. QUARK!

PRAWNBAUM. I wasn't.

INTERVIEWER. I'm so sorry. Please continue.

PRAWNBAUM. Well, as I was saying, the worker bees do have a much longer life.

INTERVIEWER. QUARK!

PRAWNBAUM. I'm sorry, I didn't mean to say 'life'. It's just that you've got me rather rattled.

INTERVIEWER. SH!

PRAWNBAUM. But this is how the bee community works.

INTERVIEWER. SH!

PRAWNBAUM. The queen bee –

INTERVIEWER. SH!

PRAWNBAUM. – stays in the hive –

INTERVIEWER. PPWP! (Short raspberry.) PWP.

PRAWNBAUM. Was that because I said 'hive'?

INTERVIEWER. Pardon? SH!

PRAWNBAUM. Did you make that noise because I said 'hive'?

INTERVIEWER. Oh, no, no, no.

PRAWNBAUM. Well, why did you make it then?

INTERVIEWER. I was just practising.

PRAWNBAUM. Practising?

INTERVIEWER. Practising for a word you're bound to say very soon. Do go on.

PRAWNBAUM. Well, the worker bees –

INTERVIEWER. SSH.

PRAWNBAUM (pause). – fly from flower to flower –

INTERVIEWER. SSH.

PRAWNBAUM (pause). – collecting –

INTERVIEWER. SSH.

PRAWNBAUM (pause). – the –

INTERVIEWER. SH.

PRAWNBAUM. – pollen.

INTERVIEWER. PWP.

PRAWNBAUM. I see. Pollen.

INTERVIEWER. PWP.

PRAWNBAUM. Pollen, pollen, pollen.

INTERVIEWER. PWP. PWP. PWP.

PRAWNBAUM. I mean, this is the stupidest thing I've ever heard in my life!

INTERVIEWER. QUARK.

PRAWNBAUM. Every time I say 'pollen' or 'hive' –

INTERVIEWER. SSH.

PRAWNBAUM. – or 'life' –

INTERVIEWER. QUARK.

PRAWNBAUM. How did you ever become an interviewer? (INTERVIEWER starts running in circles around PRAWNBAUM.) What's going on now? Is this because I said 'interviewer'? Interviewer! Interviewer! Interviewer! Interviewer! Interviewer! Interviewer! Interviewer! Interviewer! (INTERVIEWER falls into orchestra pit. Pause.) Well, we certainly know a little bit more about bees. And next on Nationwide tonight, we look at another aspect of life.

INTERVIEWER (from pit). QUARK. PWP! PWP! PWP! SSH! QUARK! QUARK! QUARK!

This sketch is great fun to read aloud at home (or in any of the world's major prisons).

If you're playing Prawnbaum and are having difficulty pronouncing 'PPWP' we recommend you try Bangalore Foul Mutton or any vindaloo dish before reading.

PRAWNBAUM shoots him twice. He dies.

What's On in Stoke Newington

ALEXEI SAYLE

A Biographical Note by the Programme Note People

Alexei is terribly nice really, though he asked us not to say so. When he's not writing this filth he likes nothing more than to curl up on a sofa with a Beatrix Potter book or a really good biography of Jim Prior.

After leaving Eton and the Guards, Alexei trained to be a stockbroker by banging his head repeatedly against hard steel surfaces. But despite terrible injuries he was still found to be too basically intelligent for the work, and he took to street theatre.

His first play, <u>Got Yer!</u>, was premiered in Stoke Newington High Street. Sayle played Alexei the young hoodlum who ran up behind old ladies, bashed them over the head and grabbed their handbag. With the help of an Arts Council grant Sayle was able to afford a No. 1 'Kwik-Bash' no-sound jemmy. The play ran for three performances in Stoke Newington before being transferred to Parkhurst.

Alexei describes himself as a radical independent. Both his feet are left.

I'm actually a journalist. I'm gossip columnist on What's On in Stoke Newington. You might have seen it, it's a big piece of paper with 'Fuck all' written on it. It's great, Stoke Newington, actually. We've several very interesting kinds of cystitis going round . . . It's great stuff, this cystitis; in fact, we've just formed Cystitis Sufferers Against the Nazis. We had a march the other day. (Well, it was more of a mince, actually, going, 'Ooh, fuck, ooh, aah aah . . .') I think it did a lot of good, you know. Actually, the life-style in Stoke Newington is terribly alternative, you know. I mean, everybody is growing their own denim, you know. I actually knit my own yogurt. It's really 'tastic, you know. (Love your poncho, by the way.) I've been on my holidays this year, went to a Greek island Domestos, you know. . .

The scene is terribly alternative, but there is one thing about the scene I cannot get behind and that is all the people taking drugs – and not giving me any, the bastards! I think, if you want to get out of your head, what's wrong with going out and having ninety-three pints, of real ale, you know, Scruttock's Old Dirigible with the twigs and bits of beak still in it, you know, and the chunky jumper and a suit with a tailored pocket for a calculator, all telling racy stories about commodity investment. 'Nyah, nyah, nyah . . .'. They're not called wine bars because of what they drink, it's what they fucking do: whine all the time! 'Nyah, nyah, nyah . . .' ('Oh, the quiche looks rather nice . . .' 'Seen the latest Woody Allen film? Awful, isn't it?' 'Ever had a multiple orgasm? Awful, isn't it?')

I'm going to sing a folk-song for you now. It's about whale smuggling in the nineteenth century and it was written by a civil servant three weeks ago. Here we go now...

Rickety-too
Rickety-too
Rickety-toodle-oodle-oo...

Can you imagine the folk-songs they're going to be singing in a hundred years' time, you know, like –

Oh, I am a computer programmer
From jolly Milton Keynes.
On weekdays I wear a suit
But at the weekend Fiorucci jeans
'Tis my delight on a Friday night
To cook some haricot beans
In my tracksuit
With rollerskates on
And one of them stupid fucking Sony
headphone units...

(Deaf-aids for trendies.)
You do all that, right, and then you round off the evening with a tortoise vindaloo ... in the half shell. 'Ah, good evening, sir, and what would you like to throw up tonight?' 'Well, I think the chicken biriani with the pilau fried rice; make a nice kind of Pointillistic pattern on the floor.' (I tell you, if you go around New Delhi at closing time – the streets are full of millions of pissed Indians throwing up steak and kidney pies...)
I went round to some friends' flat the other night, you know. I got up to the flat, right, and I noticed this sickly sweet smell, sickly sweet bloody smell. I thought, 'Aye aye, spam for tea.' Then I saw them, the extra long nine-skin Gauloise dick compensators they was rolling. I said, 'Byron, how did you manage to get the spam in there?'
Then I realized what was happening, I said I'm hip to this groove, daddy-o, twenty-three skidoo, rock-around-the-crocodile man ... so they all ignored me, you know. I sat down on the Habitat pine scatter cushions, they all settled down for a good alternative night in, you know, lentil fondue bubbling away on the hot plate. ('Oh yes, got this recipe out of a book called A Thousand and One Things to do with Cling Peaches' – or a thousand and two if you eat the fuckers.) And they put the child into his Victorian night smock ... made him look like an extra from Tess of the D'Urbervilles. They're all sitting there with teacosies on their heads, telephone coil wire coming out of them. They're all weekend white Rastafarians, living on the front line in Hemel Hempstead.

This one guy said, 'This is really amazing dope, you know, I mean it's really incredible, man. I mean, it's really amaaaazing,' he said. 'Well let me tell you about some dope I had the other week. It was really good stuff; it was Swedish leb, you know. Just one toke of this dope, just one toke – I was paralysed from the waist down, I lost the use of my fingers, I developed every single symptom of typhoid! It was fucking amaaaazing!'

They're all going, 'Oh, fucking amazing,' 'Oh fucking fantastic,' 'Oh, save the shrimp, man.'

This second guy, right, another civil servant, says, 'Actually, I've been taking coke, you know, cocaine. It's really good stuff, it's only about nine-fifths Harpic, you know it's TFM, you know – it's too fucking much. You know, I had one snort of this coke, right, just one snort, and I went blind for a fortnight. It was fucking amaaaazing!'

And they're all going, 'Oh, fucking amazing,' 'Oh, fucking fantastic,' 'Oh, save the Morris Minor, man . . .' (A Morris Minor's like being inside a fifties radio, isn't it? See them all, peddling away . . . 'Look, look, it's Noddy the social worker!' Cunt!)

This first guy's a bit pissed off, so he says, 'OK, stakes are raised. I've been taking napalm. I've been roasting the phone in the oven, then taking it through my kneecaps. I've been taking acid, you know. I dropped a couple of tabs round at Kenny and Dave's, you know, round the squat, you know. It's really nice there; they're making an effort – they're using a pig on a string as an airfreshener . . . It was really amazing acid, you know, it was much better than Sainsbury's tinned creamed magic mushrooms . . . You see, we dropped these two tabs, you know, and our brains started to throb. I didn't think Kenny and Dave had any brains left after Knebworth . . .'.

Well, who fucking would have! Nine fucking hours of Santana, eighteen quid for a fucking lentilburger. It was like the First World War. Of course, they had heavy metal then but it was called shrapnel in those days. Oh, actually it was wonderful, Knebworth. Remember that wonderful climactic moment when we all struck a match and held it aloft, you know. Suddenly there was fifty thousand people going, 'Oww fucking 'ell . . .'

Where you are allowed to say 'fucking' in Britain today

(i) At home

(ii) At work

(iii) At the pub

(iv) In the car

(v) At a football match

(vi) At a party

(vii) With your mates

Where you are not allowed to say 'fucking' in Britain today

(i) on Celebrity Squares

(ii) On The Archers

(iii) On the news

(iv) In the newspapers

(v) On BBC radio

(vi) On BBC TV

(vii) On ITN sport

(ix) On ITN news

(x) On the Queen's Christmas message

Death on the Roads

Jasper is at his best in front
of a full house. Here he is
performing in the livingroom
of no. 18 Arbroath Avenue
at Christmas 1963

AUSTRALIAN MOTOR INSURANCE CLAIMS

Some of you may be aware of the fact that for quite a number of years now I have been collecting motor insurance claim form statements. I found some more in Australia. For those of you who aren't in the know, what happens is, if you have an accident, you know, on your car or bike or something, the insurance company sends you a claim form. It's a pretty stupid claim form – lots of silly questions like what's your name, where do you live. . . Well, they've sent you the damn form. . . Things like, 'How fast were you going at the time of the accident?' and everybody writes, 'Twenty-eight miles per hour.' On the back is a big empty space and it says at the top, 'Give in your own words a description of how the accident occurred.' And these are what people have genuinely written on their claim forms and sent into this insurance office. I'll just do a few English ones first to give you some idea of how it goes. They write things like, 'I ran into a stationary tree coming in the other direction.'

'I bumped into a lamp post which was obscured by human beings.'

'Coming home, I drove into the wrong house and collided with a tree I haven't got.'

'The accident was caused by me waving to the man I hit last week.'

'I knocked over a man. He admitted it was his fault as he had been knocked down before.' . . .

Much to my delight, they have exactly the same system in operation in Australia as we do, and people write more or less the same sort of things as we do – only much better. These are Australian motor insurance claim form statements: 'The pedestrian had no idea which direction to run, so I ran over him.'

'I told the police I was not injured, but on removing my hat I found I had a fractured skull.'

'The bloke was all over the road, I had to swerve a number of times before I hit him.'

'I had been driving for forty years when I fell asleep at the wheel.'

And this is my all-time favourite: 'I saw a slow-moving, sad-faced old gentleman as he bounced off the bonnet of my car.'

Last year alone one thousand eight hundred and fourteen Frenchmen were killed on the roads. In Germany the toll was even higher: two thousand and five; in Italy, higher still: two thousand four hundred and seventy; whilst in Spain, the highest of all, a staggering three thousand nine hundred and twenty seven. Now I'm telling you this because many of you here tonight could be taking your cars to the continent on holiday this year. These figures concern you directly. Now it's easy to say, 'I'm not surprised, the way they drive' but you know that's not the point. The one thing that should strike you about these figures is this. Alarming as they are, they are just not enough.

There are over sixty million dagos in Spain. Four thousand just doesn't register. I'm sorry. And there are even more krauts, froggies and slimy wops polluting the highways of Europe. Now you might say, 'Well, what can I do?' with a helpless shrug of the shoulders. Well, I'll tell you what you can do. When you go to the continent on holiday this year, remember you are British. Therefore drive on the left-hand side of the road. Keep to the good old British laws. Or at least some of them. Let's have none of this priorité à droite rubbish in these froggie countries. If you're in the middle of Paris, Madrid, Munich or Rome and you don't know whether you're coming or going, just stick your foot down and go like hell in a straight line. You'll get through! You'll get through! As a general rule when touring the continent, if there's any doubt what-soever, go that way.

And don't let this stop at Calais. If you should come across an alien on one of our motorways, for instance, try nudging him off. It makes a really great family outing on a Sunday afternoon to see a load of Luxembourgeois shaking their fists and shouting some incomprehensible gibberish as they go rolling gently over the hard shoulder and down the embankment. Now I would be the last to deny that these activities involve some element of risk. But what true-blooded Briton could possibly resist such a call from his mother country? Above all, remember, take some of them with you.

What can one say about Rowan Atkinson

that hasn't been said already?

Well, one can say that he once

took off Princess Margaret's knickers

and ran the length of Greek Street with

them over his head.

But why bother?

The Royal Australian Prostate Foundation

'At last! A performer with the wit, vivacity and style to put the fun back into intestinal operations. To those of us who suffered for so long with a grumbling appendix or a hypercritical pancreas, Dame Edna is as fresh as a new box of Rennies.'

<u>The Abdominal Weekly</u>

'Australian humour at its very best.'

David Niven

My name is Dame Edna Everage, housewife, superstar, mother, megastar and Melbourne millionairess. I wasn't sure about this little Amnesty night because I generally support my own special pet little charity, which is the very very wonderful Royal Australian Prostate Foundation.

My husband, Norm, well he hasn't been a well man. I've had his prostate hanging over my head for many years, and for a very long time, the poor darling, he has had a rumbling prostate, but he never let on, he's kept it under his hat, particularly at the pictures. But it had to leak out in the end; it did, and, you know, there is a wonderful new operation which thanks to my munificence we have been exploring in Australia. It's a part of the branch of cyrogenics where they snap-freeze the prostate in the hope that one day a doctor or a wonderful surgeon will be born who can perform a miracle operation. But of course this is cold comfort to my husband in more ways than one.

Oh silly billy me, I had to take it home from the hozzie in a thermos on the back seat of my car, and I can assure you that I haven't had Norm's organ there for many moons, and then I got it home and I've tucked it in the freezing compartment of our fridge. It's there on the left at the back. I've got all the barbie meat on the right. My worry, of course, is that my marvellous old bridesmaid, Madge Allsop, will get a little bit peckish in the middle of the night. She could be in the mood for a scrummy old shish-kebab, couldn't she, darlings? I could come home from one of these lovely shows that I do and find my husband's organ halfway down her throat. That's a worry, but it is lovely for me to be here because I am a believer in Amnesty. You know, in Australia half the population are behind bars, they are, and the other half are leaning on them, my darlings . . .

This little frock, of course, the little smart trend-setters in the audience will be up all night copying, I know that. They will be, they will be. Little Thea Porter will be huddled over her Singer all night, won't she, copying this lovely frock of mine which is inspired by the Sydney Opera House casino. Can you see it? It's just dawned on you, you poor little things, saturated with satire that you are. A little bit of naturalness comes as a bit of a shock to you I suppose – does it?

But to me, when I do my little sharing shows, it's not just me, it's you as well. I know that sounds a sentimental silly old thing, but that's the kind of person I am. I'm a bit of an old softy – I'm an old softy from way back, darlings, and it's the public that mean such a lot to me and I feel a little song coming on . . .

A cheering crowd at my stage-door
An audience crying out for more
That's what my public means to me
The loyal fans who queue for hours
The cards, the telegrams and all those lovely
    flowers
Yes, and that's what my public means to me
You need to have a pretty humble attitude
When you see little faces looking up grotesque
    with gratitude
But from tiny tots to grannies
I love all your nooks and crannies
That's what my public means to me

The Queen's birthday honours list
This lovely Cartier on my wrist
That's what my public means to me
A limousine, a sable coat
The lump that's rising in my throat
That's what my public means to me
Superstars may come and go but there's no other
The folks identify with their own mother
To think there's people in this room
Who wished they'd sprung out of my womb*
That's what my public means to me

The royal visitors who call
A concert in the Alfred Hall
That's what my public means to me
All those requests I get to stay
With famous folk in St Tropez
That's their idea of fun for me
But you can keep Roman Polanski
    and Bianca
It's for the company of nobodies like
    you I hanker
You're my shelter from the storm
You're as precious as my Norm
That's what my public means to me

And now the time has come to pass
I feel a lump inside my . . . heart
That's what my public do to me
The little know-alls squirt their poison
I can feel my eyelids moisten
But I know that my public stills stands true to me
I may be forced to live in a tax haven
But I know I'm poor when I see all those gladdies
    waving
And how could I forsake them
When they raise their stalks and wave them
That's what my public means to me

Thank you, darlings, thank you.

*That's not a word you often hear in a song, is it, darlings?

Musical Interlude

THE UNIVERSAL SOLDIER

He's five foot two, and he's six feet four
He fights with missiles and with spears
He's all of thirty-one, and he's only seventeen
Been a soldier for a thousand years

He's a Catholic, a Hindu, an atheist, a Jain
A Buddhist and a Baptist, and a Jew
And he knows he shouldn't kill
And he knows he always will
Kill you for me, my friend
And me for you

And he's fighting for Canada
He's fighting for France
He's fighting for the USA
And he's fighting for the Russians
And he's fighting for Japan
And he thinks we'll put an end to war this way

And he's fighting for democracy
He's fighting for the Reds
He says it's for the peace of us all
He's the one who must decide
Who's to live and who's to die
And he never sees the writing on the wall

But without him how would Hitler have condemned him in the war
Without him Caesar would have stood alone
He's the one who must decide
Who's to live and who's to die
And without him all this killing can't go on

He's the Universal Soldier, and he really is to blame
His orders come from far away no more
They come from here and there
And you and me
And brothers, can't you see
This is not the way we put the end to war

Donovan is sitting on the same seat
as Jasper Carrott.
— Pointless   ed.

We thought that's what
'Programme Notes' were all about.
Palin & Jones

— Sorry, but if we just wanted
that sort of stuff, we could have
got John Cleese to do it — ed.

This is Bob Geldof at it. They were very lucky to get him as he is in very big demand over VAT invoices and various other irregularities. But it's to his credit that he not only turned up but also brought a bag of crisps.

I DON'T LIKE MONDAYS

The silicon chip inside her head gets switched to overload
And nobody's going to go to school today
She's going to make them stay at home
And daddy doesn't understand it
He always said she was as good as gold
And he can see no reasons
Cos there are no reasons
What reason do you need to be sure

Tell me why
I don't like Mondays
Tell me why
I don't like Mondays
Tell me why
I don't like Mondays
I want to shoot the whole day down

The telex machine is kept so clean
And it types to a waiting world
And mother feels so shocked
Father's world is rocked
And their thoughts turn to their own little girl
Sweet sixteen, ain't that peachy keen
But it ain't so neat to admit defeat
They can see no reasons
Cos there are no reasons
What reasons do you need

Tell me why
I don't like Mondays
Tell me why
I don't like Mondays
Tell me why
I don't like Mondays
I want to shoot the whole day down

And now the playing's stopped in the playground now
She wants to play with her toys awhile
And school's out early and soon we'll be learning
And the lesson today is 'How to Die'
And then the bullhorn crackles
And the captain tackles with the problems and the hows and whys
And he can see no reasons
Cos there are no reasons
What reasons do you need to die

And the silicon chip inside her head gets switched to overload
And nobody's going to go to school today
She's going to make them stay at home
And daddy doesn't understand it
He always said she was as good as gold
And he can see no reasons
Cos there are no reasons
What reason do you need to be sure

Tell me why
I don't like Mondays
Tell me why
I don't like Mondays
Tell me why
I don't like Mondays
Tell me why
I don't like Mondays
Tell me why
I don't like Mondays
I want to shoot the whole day down

FARTHER UP THE ROAD

Farther on up the road
Someone's gonna hurt you like you hurt me
Farther on up the road
Someone's gonna hurt you like you hurt me
Farther on up the road
Baby, you just wait and see

You got to reap just what you sow
That old saying is true
You got to reap just what you sow
That old saying is true
Just like you mistreat someone
Someone's gonna mistreat you

Now you're laughing, pretty baby
Someday you're gonna be crying
Now you're laughing, pretty baby
Someday you're gonna be crying
Farther on up the road
You'll find out I wasn't lying

Farther on up the road
When you're alone and blue
Farther on up the road
When you're alone and blue
You're gonna ask me to take you back
But I'll have somebody new

THE IMMORTALS

Jeff and Eric together on stage for the first time since _Babes in the Wood_ at the Hackney Palace.

Performers of such international repute that John Cleese thought they came from a car hire firm.

STAGE FRIGHT: A DOCTOR WRITES

What Phil Collins is experiencing here is a condition known to anyone who has had to appear on a public stage. Henry Irving, Donald Wolfit, Sarah Bernhardt, Sir Ralph Richardson - all had the shits at some time in their career.

It can only be cured by joining Actors Equity or stuffing something up your bum.

IN THE AIR TONIGHT

I can feel it coming in the air tonight, oh Lord
I've been waiting for this moment, all my life, oh Lord
Can you feel it coming in the air tonight, oh Lord, oh Lord

Well if you told me you were drowning
I would not lend a hand
I've seen your face before, my friend
But I don't know if you know who I am
Well, I was there and I saw what you did
I saw it with my own two eyes
So you can wipe off that grin
I know where you've been
It's all been a pack of lies

And I can feel it coming in the air tonight, oh Lord
Well I've been waiting for this moment for all my life, oh Lord
I can feel it in the air tonight, oh Lord, oh Lord
I've been waiting for this moment for all my life, oh Lord, oh Lord

Well I remember
I remember, don't worry
How could I ever forget
It's the first time
And the last time that we ever met
But I know the reason why you keep your silence up
No, you don't fool me
'Cause the hurt doesn't show
And the pain still grows
It's no stranger to you and me

I can feel it coming in the air tonight, oh Lord
I've been waiting for this moment for all my life, oh Lord
I can feel it coming in the air tonight, oh Lord, oh Lord
I've been waiting for this moment for all my life, oh Lord

MESSAGE IN A BOTTLE

Just a castaway
An island lost at sea – o
Another lonely day
With no one here but me – o
More loneliness than any man could bear
Rescue me before I fall into despair – o

I'll send an SOS to the world
I'll send an SOS to the world
I hope that someone gets my
I hope that someone gets my
I hope that someone gets my
Message in a bottle
Message in a bottle
Message in a bottle
Message in a bottle

A year has passed since I wrote my note
I should have known this right from the start
Only hope can keep me together
Love can mend your life
But love can break your heart

I'll send an SOS to the world
I'll send an SOS to the world
I hope that someone gets my
I hope that someone gets my
I hope that someone gets my
Message in a bottle
Message in a bottle
Message in a bottle

I don't believe what I saw
A hundred billion bottles
Washed up on the shore
Seems I'm not alone in being alone
A hundred billion castaways looking
for a home

I'll send an SOS to the world
I'll send an SOS to the world
I hope that someone gets my
I hope that someone gets my
I hope that someone gets my
Message in a bottle
Message in a bottle
Message in a bottle
Message in a bottle

Sending out an SOS
Sending out an SOS
Sending out an SOS
Sending out an SOS

This is NOT a pull-out supplement of the superstar STING.
If you want to stick it on the wall of your bedroom or cell, you will have to pin the ENTIRE BOOK up on the wall. If you try to pull STING out the book will fall apart.
PTO for his legs.

ROXANNE

Roxanne
You don't have to put on the red light
Those days are over
You don't have to sell your body to the night

Roxanne
You don't have to wear that dress tonight
Walk the streets for money
You don't care if it's wrong or if it's right

Roxanne
You don't have to put on the red light
Roxanne
You don't have to put on the red light

I loved you since I knew you
I wouldn't talk down to you
I have to tell you just how I feel
I won't share you with another boy

You know my mind is made up
So put away your make-up
Told you once, I won't tell you again
It's a bad way

Roxanne
You don't have to put on the red light
Roxanne
You don't have to put on the red light
Put on the red light
Put on the red light

I loved you since I knew you
I wouldn't talk down to you
I have to tell you just how I feel
I won't share you with another boy

You know my mind is made up
So put away your make-up
Told you once, I won't tell you again
It's a bad way

Roxanne
You don't have to put on the red light
Roxanne
You don't have to put on the red light
Put on the red light
Put on the red light
Put on the red light
You don't have to put on the red light
Roxanne
Roxanne
Roxanne
Roxanne

Throughout his life STING has nurtured an ambition to appear on page 54 of a book. He applied unsuccessfully for page 54 of *The French Lieutenant's Woman*, was beaten to it by Mrs Murdstone in *David Copperfield*, but at last, thanks to a generous financial offer to the editors, he achieves his ambition.

Top of the Form

CAST

Question Master	.	.	.	John Cleese

The Boys

Brian	.	.	.	. Rowan Atkinson
Kevin	.	.	.	. John Fortune
Stig	.	.	.	. Griff Rhys Jones

The Girls

Tracey	.	.	.	. Tim Brooke-Taylor
Arthura	.	.	.	. John Bird
Cynthia	.	.	.	. Graham Chapman

The QUESTION MASTER sits in the middle with three boys on one side and three girls on the other.

SATIRE!

QUESTION MASTER. Hello, good evening and welcome to another edition of Top of the Form. And this week we're at the semi-final stage and tonight's contest is between the boys of the King Arthur's Grammar School, Podmoor and the girls of the St Maria Kangarooboot the Second County High School and a Half. (Quick unnatural applause).
And so, without further ado, let's go straight on with round two. Brian, what is the name of the meat that we get from pigs?

BRIAN. Pork.

QUESTION MASTER. Good, that's two marks to you, Brian. Tracey, what is the name of the metal alloy we get from zinc and copper?

TRACEY. Brass.

QUESTION MASTER. No, no, I'm afraid not, the answer's pork. Kevin, what is the capital of Australia?

KEVIN. Sydney.

QUESTION MASTER. No, no, the capital of Australia is pork. Now, Arthura, who wrote A Tale of Two Cities?

ARTHURA. Pork.

QUESTION MASTER. Good. It's two marks to you. And so on to Stig's question. Stig, what was the date of Captain Cook's discovery of Australia?

STIG (quickly). Pork.

QUESTION MASTER. Good. Two marks to you and the last question in this round goes to you, Cynthia. Can you recite the first two lines of Thomas Gray's 'Elegy written in a country . . .'

CYNTHIA. Pork.

QUESTION MASTER. Good. Two marks to you. That's the end of round one and the score is four points to each school. (Two seconds applause.) And straight on to round two. Brian, what is the name that we give to the meat we get from pigs?

BRIAN (screaming). Pork.

QUESTION MASTER. No, no, you're guessing, aren't you? The meat we get from pigs is called Baghdad. Tracey, your question next. Tracey, what is the capital of Iraq?

TRACEY. Baghdad.

QUESTION MASTER. No. Nearly, no. The capital of Iraq is Rome. Kevin ,what is the capital of Italy?

KEVIN. Paris.

QUESTION MASTER. No, the capital of Italy is Tokyo. Arthura, what is the capital of Japan?

ARTHURA. Washington.

QUESTION MASTER. Good. Two marks to you. Stig, what is the capital of the United States of America?

STIG. Sydney.

QUESTION MASTER. Well . . .

BRIAN. Canberra.

QUESTION MASTER. Jolly good, two to you. And finally, Cynthia, what's the capital of Australia?

CYNTHIA. Pork.

QUESTION MASTER. Well done, well done indeed. And the score at the end of round two is, um (two seconds applause). And on with round three. Brian, what is the difference between a monsoon and a mongoose?

BRIAN. A mongoose is a long white plastic pole . . . which you hang out of your window to frighten the birds away . . . and a monsoon is a . . . medieval Hungarian stomach pump.

QUESTION MASTER. No, I can only give you a half for that.

BRIAN. Oh, um, Brussels, Brussels.

QUESTION MASTER. No, not Brussels. Well tried, though. No, a monsoon is a wind and a mongoose isn't. Well, that's the end of that round and the score is (two seconds applause). Now on to round four which is all about butterflies. Tracey, your question about butterflies is who wrote Jane Eyre?

TRACEY. Red admiral? Cabbage white? Fritillary?

QUESTION MASTER. No, no, you're on the wrong track here.

TRACEY. Pork.

QUESTION MASTER. No, the answer is the Taj Mahal. No, sorry, I got a bit muddled there. The answer is, in fact, Brussels, but I can give you one for cabbage white. Now that brings the score even and there's only time for one more question and whichever school gets this question right goes into the final.

ALL. Pork.

QUESTION MASTER. No, now here's the question. It's not an easy one. Ready? Now, who shuffled my question cards just before transmission?

BRIAN
STIG
KEVIN   } Tracey!
ARTHURA
CYNTHIA

. . .and the chance to dress up as schoolgirls. Lucky bitches!

QUESTION MASTER *flies at* TRACEY *and*
mutilates her with a large meat cleaver.

"I've had it up to here with Men..."

VICTORIA WOOD-TAMPAX.
leading light of the
feminist comedy revival,
and a right goer.

You can't say that
— ed.

No, alright.

Terry Jones & Michael Palin

Tampax. IUD. Pre-menstrual tension . . .

That's the feminist part of the evening over with. I'm worn out. Pamela Stephenson and me are doing our best, but these boys are very demanding: 'Suck that cock.' 'Mark that thesis.' Fortunately, they're getting on a bit. I thought backstage would be all dope and Carlsberg Special. But actually you find yourself wading knee-deep in empty Steradent tins.

When I was younger and people used to stay the night with me – that was before I got my Holly Hobby vibrator – I used to put a bolster down the middle of the bed. There's nothing odd about that, but mine had broken glass stuck in the top. Still, you do do these silly things, don't you, when you're younger? I mean, I got in with a bad crowd at school and I used to take pills, but I didn't fit in, you know, like I was the only one that had to take them crushed up in jam.

I've had it up to here with men
Perhaps I should phrase that again
Been wearing pretty dresses, floral
Taking contraceptives, oral
Since I don't remember when

I've had it up to here with blokes
And all their stupid dirty jokes
It's not a lot of fun
To hear the one about the nun
The marrow, the banana and John Noakes

It's not that I expect true love
Or gazing at the stars above
If as a person they'd acknowledge me
Not just bits of gynaecology
Or if they'd just take off their rubber gloves

To start your evenings off in Lurex
And finish them with biscuits
Doesn't really turn me on
I'll stay at home in my pyjamas
Watch a programme about llamas
I won't need any lip gloss
I won't need any Amplex
Just Ovaltine and buns for one

I've had it up to here with sex
Those nylon vests and hairy necks
They expect you to be flighty
And they act like God almighty
Cos they've got a cock and they can mend a flex

And when they proudly strip and pose
I want to stay, 'What's one of those?'
They tend to feel a failure
If you don't love their genitalia
Though why you should Christ only knows

No more nights of drinking
Nodding, smiling, thinking
'Jesus, when can I go home?'
No more struggling in taxis
In Vauxhalls, Imps and Maxis
With stupid little bleeders
With all the charming manners
Of the average garden gnome

And when they're down to socks and grin
You know it's time to get stuck in
Full of self-congratulation
They expect a combination
Of Olga Korbut, Raquel Welch and Rin Tin Tin

I've not had an encounter yet
That didn't leave me cold and wet
I'd be happier, I know
If we could only go
From the foreplay
Straight to the cigarette

I'll finish and just say again
I've definitely had it
Well, very nearly had it

Had it nearly up to here with men

At last!   A sketch with

Pamela Stephenson in it.

Solemn organ music is heard.

MINISTER. We are here to celebrate the holy
sacrament of divorce. Dennis, wilt thou leave this
woman, who is thy wedded wife? Dost thou dislike
her, despise her, has thou told her a thousand times
if thou've told her once to squeeze the toothpaste
tube from the bottom and not the top and dost thou

despise her brother, the chartered surveyor, who invites himself to dinner and then drinks thy Scotch after ye have gone to bed? Dost thou dislike her mother, hate her cooking, get irritated that she picks at her toenails in bed, and that the clippings somehow find their way into that little crack in the side of the duvet, and wilt thou forsake her for as long as ye both shall live?

DENNIS. I will.

MINISTER. Muriel, wilt thou leave this drunken shit who is thy wedded husband? Didst thou dislike the brevity and infrequency of his lovemaking and wert thou so sick of having to lie to him about how it's not size that's important and that you may as well be sleeping with one of those seaside collection boxes made out of a mine? Wert thou driven to distraction by the fact that he uses saucers as ashtrays and the fact that when he said he was going to his mother's for the weekend, he was in fact in Ipswich with Elsie Maynard and will you, if given half a chance, cheerfully wring his neck?

MURIEL. I will.

MINISTER. Who taketh this woman away from this man?

FRANK. I do.

MINISTER. Just say these words with me: 'I take thee from thy wedded husband.'

FRANK. I take thee from thy wedded husband.

MINISTER. 'To have and to hold, from this day forth.'

FRANK. To have and to hold, from this day forth.

MINISTER. 'For I am Frank Hodgkiss, the lounge lizard from accounts.'

FRANK. For I am Frank Hodgkiss, the lounge lizard from accounts.

MINISTER. 'And thereto I plight thee my troth.'

FRANK. And thereto I plight thee my troth.

MINISTER. Those whom I have put asunder I bet no man can join together. Dearly beloved, divorce is an honourable state and is not to be taken in hand lightly, inadvisedly or wantonly to satisfy men's carnal lusts, although that's a pretty good reason, and forasmuch as Dennis and Muriel have consented to abandon holy wedlock and instead to pledge their troth to whomsoever tickles their fancy, I pronounce that they be man and woman apart and henceforward shall be free to be swingers and frequent singles' bars that have been approved by the Archbishop of Canterbury, perhaps dancing cheek to cheek. Amen.

MURIEL. Amen.

Denis & Ronnie

Pity they couldn't get John Wells to do this because he does a better impression of Denis than Denis. Still, I suppose it was quite a scoop to get Denis himself - and he does make quite a few telling points. Nice to hear some good old-fashioned political sense in the show instead of the usual all-too-easy satirical lampooning that passes for humour these days.

I must apologize for being rather late. I have just been entertaining some frightful grubby little left-wing frog, one of Margaret's political friends apparently over here on a dirty weekend.

Amnesia is a terrible and hideous affliction. Many of my closest friends have died of terminal cases of it. But I did not know it had become international.

Nevertheless I am delighted to be here addressing my fellow members of the Mentally Retarded Rugby Football Referees Association. Here I am at least free from the attentions of the reptiles of the gutter press and the hideous TV rat-pack of closet Marxists and pinkos, always ready to sink their infected mandibles in one's fleshier parts.

I am probably unique among you in having had my retirement entirely buggered up by my wife becoming Prime Minister of Great Britain and parts of Northern Ireland. A recent poll suggests that Margaret is marginally less popular than the Black Death. I blame it on the Chancellor of the Exchequer, little Howe. I don't know whether you know him, curly hair, specs, brothel-creepers? He was quoted as saying, 'We are coming to the end of the recession.' He didn't in fact say any such thing. I was standing beside him at the time . . . a little champagne and twiglets do. He had admittedly had a tincture or twain. What he actually said was, 'We are coming to the end of the reception.'

Our main failure in my view is failing to come to grips with the unions. We came in with a rock-solid mandate, as I have frequently explained to Margaret, to club the bloody unions back into the Stone Age and who does she wheel out the moment it comes to any kind of confrontation, but Pinko Prior who is, in my humble opinion, about as much use as a one-legged man at an arse-kicking party. She really ought to take a leaf out of old Hopalong's book in Washington. Buy manacles and leg irons for every member of the TUC.

Odd thing about old Hopalong. In times of crisis, they don't bother to wake him up. In my opinion admittedly it is hardly worth it. Margaret and I saw him in Washington. There he was standing at the top of the steps, bold as brass, six inches deep in make-up, holding hands with his wife. Doesn't that strike you as very rum in a man of his age?

Meanwhile we are still threatened with the spectre of unemployment, and I myself am absolutely in favour of it. I mean, I've been unemployed for the best part of fifty-eight years. I don't go round setting fire to public vehicles and hurling Molotov cocktails at the constabulary. There's an old wrinkle from army days. If the lower ranks are getting stroppy about doing fatigues, march them out into the snow, leave them out there for a couple of nights, and they're only too grateful to come back and scrub out a nice warm shithouse.

One thing I would like to say in conclusion is this. Our present problems have been blamed by some Tory cynics on mindless hooligans bent solely on personal greed. Well, that may be true, but it's no way to talk about President Reagan and my wife.

Mind you, Denis does do a great John Wells impersonation.

Hi there, cowboys, cowgirls, cows. My Republican producers said to me, Ronnie, you're going to be a model president. I said does that mean I'm going to have some kind of big key in my back, a bunch of rich hoodlums winding me up and setting me off, left, right, left, right, left, right? They said no, if we needed that we'd have got the old Abraham Lincoln dummy out of Disneyland. Why, he talks just like you do, he has a considerably wider range of facial expressions and he did not appear in a lot of lousy 'B' movies holding hands with a chimpanzee. No, we need you for a photographic modelling assignment while we get on with running the country.

My scriptwriters and my dialogue coach have explained to me very slowly and painstakingly that I am passionately in favour of less government, which is why I have spent much of my term of office on vacation, gathering first-hand experience of unemployment and why, if there is a dogfight with the commies over the Mediterranean, or assass~ ination attempts on my person, I am usually asleep.

But that does not mean I intend to be written out of my big scene. I'm not talking about some localized nuclear conflict between two crazed, tinpot dema~ gogues like Haig and Weinberger. I mean, if it comes to real gun play, I intend to show, as a mature statesman, that I have a bigger one than any commie cocksucker over there in Pakistan, or wherever it is they come from. So we burn up a couple of billion. That's show business.

Meanwhile, as a conservative – and that does not mean I give a shit about conservation – I pledge myself to conserve, to cleanse, tone and moisturize that face of America that will, under God, strike terror into our adversaries, be they friend or foe.

Ronald Reagan doing his brilliant send up of John Wells.

Peter Shore as himself

Clothes Off!

At last! A sketch with Pamela Stephenson in it...

WOMAN. Good afternoon.

MAN. Good afternoon.

WOMAN. I am awfully sorry to trouble you, but could you possibly spare me a couple of pounds?

MAN. A couple of pounds?

WOMAN. Yes.

MAN. Oh dear, have you lost your purse?

WOMAN. No.

MAN. Could I just ask what it's for?

WOMAN. Yes, it's for me.

MAN. A couple of pounds?

WOMAN. Make it three.

MAN. Look, I'm awfully sorry, but when I left home this morning, I'm the most perfect fool, I'm afraid I went and left my wallet behind.

WOMAN. Balls.

MAN. Would you go away, please, and stop bothering me?

WOMAN. I'll do you a favour. Two pounds fifty.

MAN. Certainly not. Go away. Go on, go away or I shall call the police.

WOMAN. I think I should warn you that if you continue to be so irritating I shall be forced to take my clothes off.

MAN. I beg your pardon?

WOMAN. If you don't cough up, I'll strip.

MAN. Now, erm, look here, young lady, I'm a family
   man and I'm not accustomed to being accosted in
   the middle of the . . . What are you doing, what are
   you doing?
WOMAN. Right, there's the jacket, then.
MAN. Now look, now look, now look, now listen, now
   will you just listen to me?
WOMAN. There goes the belt.

   Skirt starts coming off.

MAN. Now, now.
WOMAN (takes off tights). There go the tights.
MAN. Now, if you – I shall call the police. Very well
   (Shouts.) Officer! Officer! Officer! This woman's not
   with me – I have never seen her before in my life.
   She's nothing to do with me.
WOMAN. Yes, I am, I'm his stepmother.
MAN. No, no, she isn't. Now look, will you just go,
   shoo, go, go, shoo. Out. Now look, I am not taking
   any more of this. Will you sh . . . oh my God. All
   right, all right three pounds, here you are.
WOMAN. No, sorry, it's gone up now. Fifty quid now.
MAN. Fifty – all right, all right. Will you take a
   cheque?
WOMAN. I've never seen you before in my life.
MAN. What?
WOMAN. Do you have some form of identification?
MAN. Identi–?

WOMAN. Right, there's the blouse then. (Shouts.) Look how he treats his stepmother, the woman who once saved him from the jaws of a crocodile. I'm waiting. Right, there's the brassière then, off with the brassière. Where's the Sunday Mirror now, eh? What are you doing?

MAN. I'm giving you a taste of your own medicine. I'm a mild man, madam, but when I'm roused there's hell to pay. (Starts to undress.) Aha!! Can't take it, eh?

WOMAN. It is not that, I . . .

MAN. Had enough?

WOMAN. All right, clover, if that's the way you want to play it.

MAN. That's the way, sugar.

WOMAN. Right. Go for your pants, big mouth!

MAN. You make the first move, sister.

WOMAN. I'm calling you, stepson.

MAN. Don't push me, blue eyes.

WOMAN. I'm pushing you, sunrise.

TOGETHER (shouting). It's the pants! It's the pants! It's the pants! etc.

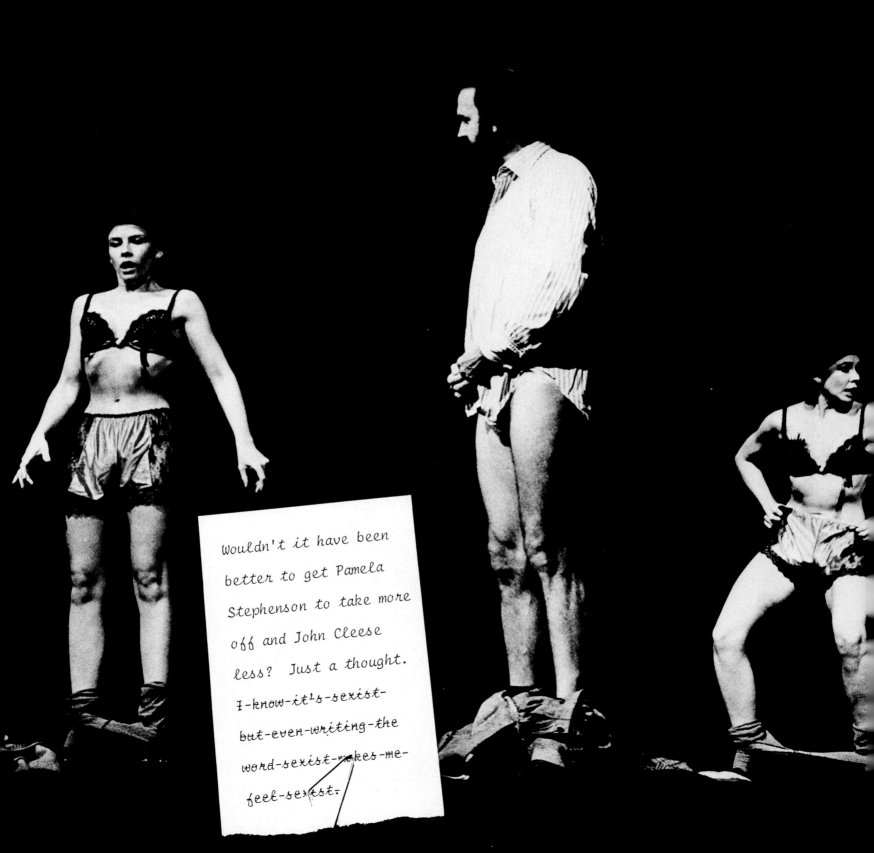

Wouldn't it have been better to get Pamela Stephenson to take more off and John Cleese less? Just a thought. ~~I-know-it's-sexist-but-even-writing-the word-sexist-makes-me-feel-sexist.~~

Enter POLICEMAN.

POLICEMAN. All right, all right, what's all this, then?

MAN. Well look, officer, you don't know me, erm . . .

POLICEMAN. All right, all right, I'm going to take you in.

MAN. No, no, certainly not. This lady and I have done nothing illegal.

WOMAN. Nothing at all.

POLICEMAN. Don't give me that, I've been watching you two. Right, now, are you coming quietly?

MAN AND WOMAN. No.

POLICEMAN. I'm going to ask you one more time. Are you coming quietly?

MAN AND WOMAN. No.

POLICEMAN. All right. It's off with the pants!

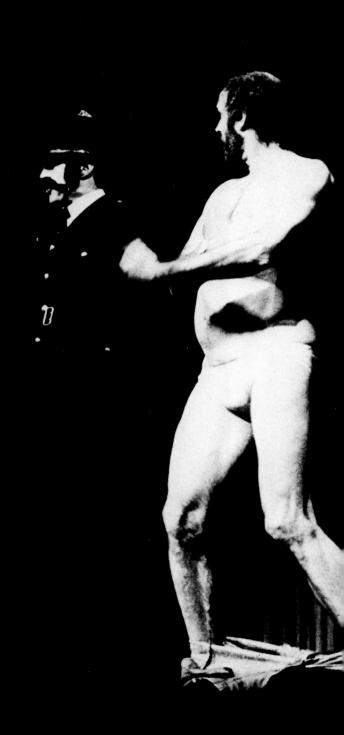

You should have seen this bit at rehearsals.

Alan & John

ALAN. And did you have to go through that tedious charade, sexual intercourse?

JOHN (eagerly). Oh yes, from A to Z.

ALAN. Z! Oh, B is the furthest I've ever wanted to go.

JOHN. Oh, no. A, B, C, D – the whole alphabet of love.

ALAN. What form did it take?

JOHN. A myriad forms.

ALAN. Put it in and jiggle it about a bit, did you?

JOHN. Well, ultimately yes, but it was a long and winding road.

ALAN. That's all it comes down to in the end, though, isn't it? Put it in and jiggle it about a bit, time after time, day in, day out. I said to my wife on the last occasion I said, 'You know, I've lost count of the number of times I've done this.' She said, 'Well, think about somebody else for a change.' 'Course I was doing – desperately. How old was she, your sex partner?

JOHN. Seventeen.

ALAN. Seventeen?

JOHN. With pert young breasts that I oh so tenderly cupped and kissed, before fondling my loving way around all the sweet highways and byways of her fresh young body.

ALAN. And then you put it in and jiggled it about. How long did it take?

JOHN. Oh, I did a real text-book job, fore-play, afterplay, all the trimmings. I don't suppose we had much change left out of three hours.

ALAN. Three hours! Jesus Christ. You could have been in Leeds in that time. Did she enjoy it?

JOHN. Oh yes, she enjoyed it all right. (Chuckles.) Oh yes, she enjoyed it all right.

ALAN. How do you know?

JOHN. Oh, the infallible sign. She started moaning. Moaning and crying, pleasure and pain inextricably mingled.

ALAN. I take all that with a pinch of salt.

JOHN. Oh no, those cries were wrenched from her very being. (Moans). 'Oh ah ah oh.' It was as though her very soul was speaking. 'Oh ah ah oh.' You know, it was almost as if she was being stabbed. In fact, I honestly did think she was being stabbed.

ALAN. Well, she was being stabbed. By you.

JOHN. Oh no, no, no. From underneath. I thought there was somebody under the bed stabbing her through the mattress. 'Oh,' she was crying, 'Oh oh oh.' In fact I was so certain that there was somebody under the bed stabbing her that I leaned right over to see if there was somebody there.

ALAN. While you were still – ?

JOHN. While I was still, yes.

ALAN. And what happened?

JOHN. She started moaning twice as much as before. She kept begging me to look under the bed again because it was so wonderful, I mean, for her.

ALAN. I think all that's put on, you know. I think it's just gone round. I think probably, once upon a time, somebody, a Mrs Wendy Barraclough, say, was laid up with a fractured pelvis and il suo marito arrived home and rather callously insisted on having his marital rights, you know –

JOHN.
ALAN. } Putting it in and jiggling it about.

ALAN. And, of course, if you have fractured your pelvis in three places, putting it in and jiggling it about a bit is acutely painful, and the hapless Wendy, of course, started moaning, you see. 'Oh ah ah oh!' and found that hubby, who was normally a reticent chartered accountant of modest sexual pretensions, was transformed into a crazed animal. So as soon as practicable she gets herself down to flower arrange- ment or whatever it is they do on an afternoon, and said, 'Listen, girls, gather round, drop the macramé – big news. If you moan they like it more; besides which it gets them to the point a lot quicker, which will leave us more time for making chutney.' Since when it's gone round, you see. One's passed it on and they're all at it now, you know, OOOH! OOOH!

JOHN. Yes. I thought she moaned because she liked me.

ALAN. Oh no. How old did you say she was?

JOHN. Seventeen.

ALAN. Oh, no, no, no, no.

JOHN. I didn't think anyone was seventeen any longer.

ALAN. Well I – more or less scored with somebody seventeen the other day.

JOHN. Oh, did you?

ALAN. Oh, yes yes.

JOHN. Oh really?

ALAN. Yes.

JOHN. Tell me about it.

ALAN. Well, I will. I was at home. It was a beautiful evening, very crisp, clear, just a hint of autumn in the air, and I thought, it's a crime to stay indoors on a night like this, so I'll just take a turn along to the lavatory at the end of Ladbroke Grove and get a breath of fresh air.

JOHN. Lavatory?

ALAN. The lavatory, yes, at the end of Ladbroke Grove.

JOHN. But you live in Ladbroke Grove.

ALAN. I do live in Ladbroke Grove, yes, I do.

JOHN. Was there some sort of malfunction with your own toilet?

ALAN. No, no, at last flush it was in tip-top condition. Do you know that lavatory at all?

JOHN. Well, yes. I mean, I – I – I have been there on occasion, I mean, you know, purely for functional reasons.

ALAN. Yes, yes, of course. Well, that's why most people go, you see, they go for absolutely pure legal and – and – functional reasons, I mean, for the purpose for which it is designed, you see. I don't. I go for . . . ancillary reasons.

JOHN. I – I – I – didn't know that.

ALAN. No, well, you wouldn't know that, because I haven't come out of the closet.

JOHN. In Ladbroke Grove?

ALAN. No, I've gone into the closet in Ladbroke Grove.

JOHN. Oh, into it. Well, I see.

ALAN. I was speaking metaphorically, you see, but it's a very reliable sort of place, really. It's not three-star, but it's quite definitely two crossed knives and forks. It's got a very eclectic clientele; you get a very good social mix. There's the usual groundswell of Spanish waiters, one or two BBC, a sprinkling of Foreign Office, and, God bless Our Lady of Downing Street, many, many unemployed youths.

JOHN. Unemployed youths?

ALAN. Yes, yes, many of them. Great pity, but there they are.

JOHN. Dreadful, tragic.

ALAN. Anyway, I've stood, you see, in the toilet purporting to have a Jimmy Riddle for about twenty minutes.

JOHN. Twenty minutes?

ALAN. Yes, twenty minutes, yes.

JOHN. Is that what you have to do?

ALAN. Oh yes, you have to do that. It's a real RSC award-winning performance, really. I mean, in any other context it would get you a Tony or an Oscar, and indeed in that context occasionally gets you a Tony, less often an Oscar. Anyway, I'm stood there, you see, and meanwhile various good citizens come and go, having emptied their honest bladders, but very very quiet, nothing happening, not a nibble. Probably a Bette Davis movie on television, or something like that. Then, suddenly, the doorway is darkened by the massive form of Mr Right.

JOHN. Mr Right?

ALAN. Mr Right. I mean, six foot tall, bronzed, blonde, crisp hyacinthine curls, built . . . like a brick shithouse and, biggest plus of all, never says a word.

JOHN. Never says a word?

ALAN. Never says a word. You see, the beauty of which is, . . . allows me free play with all my fantasies.

JOHN. Of course.

ALAN. Yes and I thought, is he a Hungarian truck driver, fresh from driving his juggernaut across the motorways of Europe and to hell with the environment? Is he, oh, a member of the SAS, with his balaclava dangling nonchalantly from his back pocket? Ah –

JOHN. Is he the Waynefleete Professor of Moral Philosophy in the University of Oxford?

ALAN. No, that hadn't really occurred to me.

JOHN. No, no.

ALAN. It wasn't, anyway, I don't think, no. Anyway, dissolve to half an hour later. We're back at my place, my wife is upstairs somewhere, making her four hundred and thirty seventh quiche of the day, and we're downstairs in the snug.

JOHN. The rumpus room?

ALAN. The rumpus room, yes. We're just about to cross the start line. I'd eased down his nether garments with practiced skill and he has done the same for me with a clumsiness I found rather endearing. It's at this point that doubts begin to creep in, because, to begin with, he seems totally – ah – unfamiliar with the geography of the area in question and, while what I've got to offer is respectable, it's not remarkable, but he's gazing upon it with all the wonder of an eskimo gazing at the Eiffel Tower.

JOHN. Silent upon a peak in Darien.

ALAN. Exactly yes, yes. And it's then that the thought strikes me, la pensée and it's a pensée that certainly never occurred to Pascal, or if it did, he certainly didn't publish it. This bugger is a policeman.

JOHN. So what did you do?

ALAN. Well, I taxed him with it. I said, 'You've seen one of those before, I suppose? Ha, ha.'

JOHN. Irony?

ALAN. You're not unfamiliar with it.

JOHN. Litotes.

ALAN. Exactly, and I said to him, 'Are you a policeman?' and he said, 'No, actually, I'm more familiar with feet. I'm a chiropody student at Richmond Polytechnic,' so I went right off it, really. Not my cup of tea at all. But he was seventeen.

JOHN. And he didn't – moan?

ALAN. Oh, no no no no. Boys don't moan, you see. Well, I mean they moan about not having a job or not having anywhere to sleep or, you know, not having enough money, but they don't moan about that. A little grunt is the most you'll ever get.

JOHN. Well, I suppose it is all in the mind.

ALAN. Oh yes. And sometimes these days, not even there.

Drinking

LITTLE KNOWN FACTS OF SHOWBIZ
No. 19: Billy Connolly, ace
Scots comedian, known and loved
by his friends as the Big Yin, is
in fact the fourth of the Grade
Brothers. Born Billy Winogradski
in the Baltic town of Riga
43 years ago, he changed his
name to Wilf Shipyardworker,
Harry Milkman and Ron Truckdriver
before going into show business
as Les Vomit the Pavement Artist.
But despite his 'naughty' jokes
and references to a bit of Jasper
Carrott coming up every time you're
sick, his brothers say if he comes
back he can have a TV channel.

I'm going to talk to you about drinking. Apart from being my hobby, it's my country's national sport. And it's funny, we don't have any drinking songs. The English have a lot of drinking songs, you know, all that stuff about 'Here's good luck to the barrel' and 'John Barleycorn' and all that, but in Scotland we don't have that. I think by the time we get around to singing we're too pissed to write songs. So we've got hangover songs...

There's this guy who lives beside me in Scotland. He's a heavier drinker than me and he makes me feel like a moderate drinker. This guy's got cirrhosis of the face. His hand's just a blur and his wee wife never drinks, never drank in her life until last Christmas. She came into the local. He said, 'Now come on, have a wee drink.'

'Come on, your lunch is ready.'

'No, have a wee drink, a drink never hurt anybody.'

'No, I don't. You know I don't.'

'Come on, you're attracting attention to me. Just one. Anything. Name it, you got it. Except advocaat; I'm not buying advocaat, OK? It's a bottle of snot. I wouldn't buy you that. How can people drink that? The drunkard's omelette.'

'Oh, I don't know, just get me the same as you.'

'Large whisky and ale, John! Now get that down you.'

Now, I don't know if you can remember the first time you tasted whisky; it's a kind of shock to the system. In Scotland it usually happens when you're four. Not that your parents give it to you. It's usually at Hogmanay or New Year time when all your relatives are in the house singing songs. Scotsmen have a great habit of singing about being away when they're there...

'Bonny Scotland, I adore thee, though I'm far across the sea...'

'What are you talking about? You're in the living room.'

'Shut up, you; it's the only song your father knows right through.'

And Uncle Willie always turns up pissed, leans on the mantelpiece, slides along and breaks all the ornaments.

I've been to some crackers, let me tell you. I've been to some splendid parties. You don't get eyes like that reading the Daily Mirror. (And I'm not a junkie; I'm really this old.) I was at a party once at Springburn in Glasgow and I've never seen anything like it in my life. It was wall to wall piss artists, all singing different songs, crunching glass underfoot – a great time. And I was talking to the guy who owned the house – he was at the fireplace with his wife – and there was a picture on the wall of a Highland soldier with bagpipes. I said, 'Is that you?'

'Aye. I was that soldier.'

'You play the pipes?'

'What, you never heard – ?'

His wife went, 'Oh, Christ, no...'

'Hold that result,' he said, and he went to the cupboard. He was throwing out cots and baby walkers and then this – thing got dragged out. It was like an octopus with pyorrhoea. He dusted it off, had a wee blow, and marched into the living room playing 'The Barren Rocks of Eden' – 'diddle ee da da da diddle ee da da' – followed by these hopeless drunks going 'Ea – sy Ea – sy!' Crunch crunch crunch crunch!

People were dancing on the coffee table, the place was going bonkers, and he did a real flashy turn at one point: 'Deedle ee da da –' and the bagpipes went whoooosh! and knocked the wedding picture off the wall – crunch, crunch! And in the middle of all this, somebody bumped into the budgie's cage. You know those ones that are up on a sort of stand? Crash. The budgie went vvooof! and came flying out like a Red Arrow, went round the room three times, and people were throwing jackets at it. 'Oooww! Get him!' And it had a heart attack, this budgie – Aaah! Crunch, crunch, crunch...

In the middle of all that, a guy arrives with forty fish suppers. 'Got youse a wee fish supper, didn't I?' He'd brought them all the way in the bus, burning his willy for the whole journey, 'ooh, aah eee aaah ooh ooh!' So to heat them up he put them in the oven in the parcel and put the gas on. There was a big pot of soup – that's a traditional Scottish thing at New Year, a big pot of soup – on top of the thing. So, 'I smell burning,' he rushed through, and this blazing parcel was dragged out. To put the flames out he threw it in the soup.

Meanwhile there's people wandering about covered in blood, because there was a bicycle in the bathroom on a pulley and the bulb wasn't working. People were staggering about; it was like the Village of the Damned. Meanwhile, there's a guy in the bedroom naked, sleeping on top of everybody's coats, and he's snoring and farting and all that... Everybody was getting embarrassed. A woman said, 'That man swore at me. I just went to get my coat and he swore at me and farted. He told me to fuck off. I don't like that kind of – '

'Who was that? Where is he? I'll get the bastard.' So he wanders in to lay waste to this guy on the bed. The man got off the bed like a dervish, with blazing eyes and filthy language, put on one shoe and kicked the guy in the balls and went back to bed. What a party! I loved it. I woke up in the morning in a different house. I didn't know anybody and I had only one shoe on.

But you see, at these parties, the ones you have at home with your aunties and uncles, all those one-eyed uncles and smelly aunties, there's always one guy who fancies himself as a real sharp singer, you know, some Uncle Bobby. He hangs about till everybody's finished and puts his glass down on the fireplace, and they always sing 'Here in my heart' and it lasts about an hour and a half.

'Heeeeere in my heaaart aaahhh hhrruuumm I'm alone and so lonely.'

'A lovely voice, there, Bob. The whole side of the family's like that.'

At that point, you wander in, four years of age, full of shortbread, sultana cake and triangular sandwiches, bored shitless, and you see the glass sitting in the fireplace; you go 'Uhhh.' Well, there's a Scottish soft drink called Irn-Bru which is the same colour as whisky, you see.

'Ooh, Irn-Bru for Bill-Bill. Aaaaaghhh!' Well, it had exactly the same effect on the woman in the pub. (Remember her? Right. That's my technique.)

She went, 'Pppphhht. Aaaarghh. Ppppphht! How can you drink this revolting, repulsive stuff?'

He says, 'See? And you think I'm out every night enjoying myself?'

For my first encore, ladies and gentlemen, I'm
not sure what I'm supposed to do, so I'll do it quick
and get the hell off because there's famous people
behind this curtain. I believe the Applejacks have re-
formed. There's a big surprise in store for you
tonight, yeah, everbody's fucked off on me. Some
bugger ran off with the T-shirt money and they're
all after him. The next act is no stranger to you.
They're walking him round the theatre all night,
trying to sober him up . . . You know that 'I'm not
pissed walk?' It's my second favourite walk.
My favourite walk is the guy at a party who knows
he's going to fart and is trying to get out of the way.
It doesn't work. All it does is divide the fart into
seven bits. You know, farting's such a strange thing.
It's an odd noise. I mean, nobody survives a noise
like that. I mean, if Hitler had farted at Nuremberg,
it would've changed the face of modern history.
Somebody was bound to laugh and find him out.
You know, when I was on tour, somebody famous
was getting divorced and it was in the paper and we
were talking about it, divorce and all that, mental
cruelty and cruel and unusual behaviour. 'I've got
this idea . . . If you loved me, you'd let me . . .
You'll get used to my little idiosyncrasies,' he said,
heating up the branding iron in the fire.

So really I reckon divorce isn't caused by these
exotic things; it's caused by smelly feet and farting
and chewing out loud, you know, eating your dinner
when it sounds like somebody running through a
swamp with their wellies full of vomit, you know?
And they grow and grow and grow, until you just
have to be separated, don't you? When you're
engaged or stepping out with a young lady, you
never fart. If you think you're going to fart, you go
away some place and then come back and blame
someone else. But when you're married . . . 'How did
you enjoy your dinner?'

'Oh it was OK.'

And lifting your leg . . .

Can you imagine how it must be, being a woman,
and you wake up freezing in the middle of the night?
Jesus, there's this thing beside you, this heaving
mass. He's been out with his pals and had nine pints
of Guinness and a vindaloo. He's got all the covers,
scratching his bollocks, farting and smiling.

'You're an animal!'

occupational hazard of
Billy Connolly's act –
cirrhosis of the
microphone

Finale:
"I Shall Be Released..."

God!

Hope it isn't significant.

I SHALL BE RELEASED

They say everything can be replaced
That every distance is not near
So I remember every face
Of every man who put me here

I see my light come shining
From the west down to the east
Any day now, any way now
I shall be released

They say every man needs protection
They say every man must fall
I can swear I can see my reflection
Some place so high above this wall

I see my light come shining
From the west down to the east
Any day now, any way now
I shall be released

Standing next to me in this lonely crowd
Is a man who swears he's not to blame
All day long I hear him screaming out so loud
He's shouting out that he was framed

I see my light come shining
From the west down to the east
Any day now, any way now
I shall be released

Oh good.

It isn't significant.

—————

Possibly a KGB agent disguised as a
double agent for M15 but actually
working for M16 (Teas Div.)

Unknown political prisoner undergoing
torture by so-called MAXPAX ?

THE SECRET POLICEMAN'S FILE

PHOTOS DISCOVERED ON
FILE AFTER THE SHOW

Possible husband and wife spy team
give secret sign while awaiting
sentence at Luton Magistrates Court
for parking offence.

A famous Welsh dissident shortly
after his arrest ?

We think these may be two SAS crack anti-terrorist storm-troopers practising community policing.

The hairy one is almost certainly working for the Icelandic Secret Service. The other is possibly an industrial spy for the White Fish Marketing Board.

B.O.S.S. agent showing I.D. card to possible black immigrant.

'M'

'N'?

The U.S. President being disguised as
a 5th-rate film actor for security
reasons.

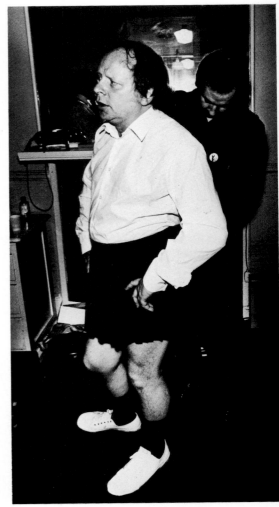

A prisoner of conscience

Pamela Stephenson and assistant
demonstrate the dangers of wanking.

Only known photo of Everly Brothers
disguised as CIA agents.

Possibly a Soviet ballet-dancer
preparing to defect back to the East.
Or possibly not.

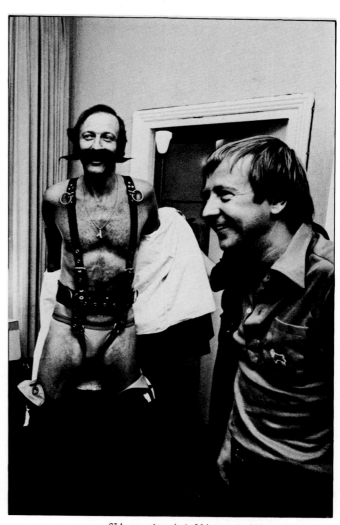

CIA counter-intelligence officer
demonstrating the latest
bullet-proof braces.

Probably an M15 (Pantos Div.) agent recruiting a mature student.

Helpful dissident tympanist frisking himself at Stornoway Airport.

Des O'Connor, Des O'Connor and Des O'Connor

Almost certainly a B.O.S.S. agent about to be blackmailed by a well-known Liberal MP.

Ex-member of the SLF (Scottish Ladies Front)

Members of the SPG arriving at the National Front Party Conference.

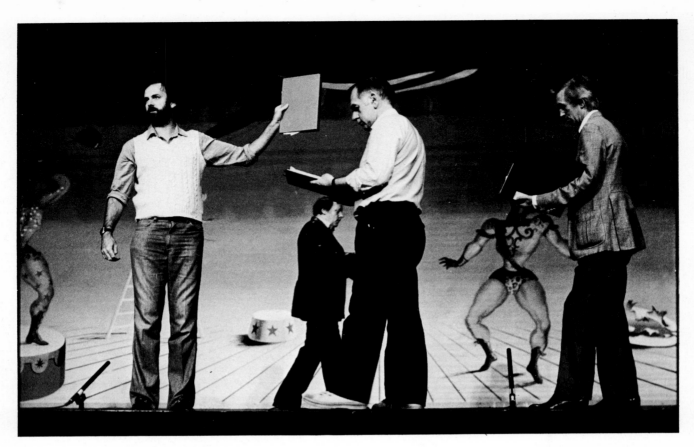

John Cleese   **Ronald Eyre**   **Michael Friend**

Design and production by Alan Kitching & Martin Lee/Birdsall & Co.
Retouching by Michael Robinson
PMTs by Bob Nichols Darkrooms
Typeset by CMS Typesetters Ltd
Reproduction by Medway Reprographic Ltd
Coffee & sandwiches by Shirley Birdsall
Photocopying by Elsa Birdsall
Printed in Great Britain by Penshurst Press Ltd

First published 1981 in Great Britain by Eyre Methuen Ltd
Reprinted November 1981
Reprinted January 1982 by Methuen London Ltd
11 New Fetter Lane, London EC4P 4EE

ISBN 0 413 50080 2